GW00692027

POEMS
FROM
THE OAK ROOM

The Cattistock Poets

FLAGON
PRESS

POEMS FROM THE OAK ROOM

Published by Flagon Press
www.flagonpress.co.uk

Foreword by Annie Freud
Edited by Annie Freud

ISBN 978-0-9562778-4-8

Poems © 2013 – Nick Morris, Maya Pieris,
Chris Slade, Marlene Sanderson, Elaine Beckett,
Liz Flight, Sarah Barr, Steve Wareham,
Lisa Storm-Olsen, Annie Freud

Designed by Andrew Crane
Typeset in Monotype Bembo
Printed by Dampier Press, Sherborne, Dorset
All rights reserved

FOREWORD

This is a selection of poems by nine members of a writing group that I have been running for the last four years. Within these pages the reader will find poems of imaginative power, boldness of intent and formal ingenuity.

All the great themes are here: rites of passage, landscape both real and metaphorical, observation of human foible, memory, love, loss and mourning.

It has been pleasure to work with these poets and to have some poems of mine published with them.

Nick Morris's ingeniously compressed poems are full of drama, sound and colour. Expect the unexpected.

Through memory and fragment, **Maya Pieris**'s tender poems are an invitation to the reader to travel into the past. The intensely personal gives way to the universal.

The influence of William Barnes may be clearly felt in **Chris Slade**'s poems, yet his treatment of rural themes is modern, fresh and ironic. In places the results are extraordinarily moving.

Marlene Sanderson's poems of a post-war childhood have a quiet dignity and demonstrate a talent for story-telling.

Elaine Beckett's accomplished poems show a finely tuned ear for the duality of human existence. These five very varied poems announce a new and original talent.

Liz Flight employs a tone that is both conversational and edgy to craft her darkly humorous and original poems.

Sarah Barr's skilful, existential poems marvellously capture a sense of malaise lurking at the heart of the conventional.

The voice in **Steve Wareham**'s poems has a refreshing exuberance and versatility. These are poems that tell the truth.

Lisa Storm-Olsen's poems have an alchemic - almost levitating - quality about them. They shimmer. This is a poet in love with language.

Annie Freud

POEMS FROM THE OAK ROOM

The Cattistock Poets

CONTENTS

NICK MORRIS

THE MURDER OF DAVID RIZZIO

Wet knives gleam in candle light.
Flintlocks at the belly of a pregnant queen.
Defiance is all she musters for a shroud;
capture this act, she gasps to herself.
The heavy corpse is kicked downstairs.
Let my blood too; it will pour down
the canvasses of painters, and down
the throats of tomorrow's balladeers.
Slowly the killers leave, their drunk
breath new incense for her faith.

ARKANSAS BLACK

It is moments after the girl walks by.
The final crumb of his wife's neatly
foiled flapjack has been eaten
and he loosens his tie's determined hold
on what he accepts as work-life balance.

This is no place for suits
He tells his reflection, fattened
in the polished skin of an apple.
He runs his thumb over its firm curves.
Its scent floats, he thinks, like love
through a younger life than his.

He stands and hurls the apple upwards.
He is twenty years younger,
the star of the first eleven, coolly
waiting to win the match, to save this
vital ruby from her fall.

The apple drops and misses his fingers,
splitting its flesh on the gravel path.
He turns with faked indifference, to check
if the girl has seen. She is walking
the other way from his office block.

LA LOGE

*after **La Loge** by Pierre-Auguste Renoir*

and what's your guess,

rented for the night?
Francs worn for petals,
a mouth that takes cuts
and hawks pleasures, smeared
with a slick of paint.

Or maybe a jewel?
polished, pert,
wide-hipped, picked
from affluent stock?
Demure, ashamed
of coercion doled out
in private mechanical rote.

Turn your eyes, as he does,
to the stage if you like
illusion scripted: white
for angels, bastards
black, vaudevillian
lust neatly cued.

Or follow his new gaze,
fixed on the box where
diamonds snigger like
trampled glass. He hopes
a powdered neck might
turn and slip the bolt
from his cage.

Then look at me longer,
and with your fingers
feel the clay rim
of the dog bowl,
lapped by countesses, brasses
and half the world, trussed
in flowered stays.

MAYA PIERIS

STAIRS

were miraculous,
allowing her to travel up and down
between people,
leaning against Dragon's back,
hanging over castle battlements,
with feet and legs
and leaping cat –
a terrain for experiments –
bouncing, sliding, dropping Teddy,
learning that raised voices always fall.

THE APPLE

It butts in – again –
the past,
pushing, poking,
into the now.

And all I was doing
was researching "The Apple"
for a talk – harmless, unimportant –
and turning to the Bible
I find it – hidden like the worm –
a letter.

And the rebuke,
mild but again
I am that child.

TITANIA AND BOTTOM
IN MONOCHROME

Turning the card
she sees the name
and cries,
no pause between reading
and reaction,
having forgotten.

She remembers
the blue paper, the ruler,
the pencil and rubber
used to mark and measure,
at constant intervals,
the lines on which to send
her love her love.

POTTING ON

I consider the plant,
lank leaves, shrunken soil,
wizened roots protruding.

I pour on water;
it seeps out:
a delta forms.

What to do,
leave alone, transplant,
uproot altogether?

CHRIS SLADE

DRONE

I have an onomatopoeic name
that sounds a little like the noise I make.
I have no sting and I am very tame.
My sisters feed me for the family's sake,
that with my sperm I may pass on their genes.
Each afternoon I fly to congregate
in places where we might meet virgin queens
and maybe have a chance to copulate.
I'm told that's where the greatest danger lies:
I guess that swallows try to snap us up.
I see their movements with my compound eyes
and don't give them a chance on me to sup.
A queen is here! I get her lovely scent!
I wonder what that danger warning meant.

I sense that virgin queen is in the mood;

a thousand other drones here think the same.

It's likely that a score will score. I'm crude:

to mount while she's a virgin is my aim!

I know that after me there will be more;

she needs her spermatheca brimming full,

but once deflowered by me she'll be a whore!

If I'm in first, she'll think I'm wonderful!

She's just upwind – I think I'm getting close.

That's her! I have her in my sight.

I'm nearest, what is there to lose?

Got her! I'll mate with all my might.

WOW!
OWW!!!

ROOT AND BRANCH

The Slades have been in Dorset
Since almost time begun.
The first time we a tax bill met
Was thirteen forty-one.

Another Slade, John he's called;
Sooner him than me,
Was hung and drawn and quartered
In fifteen eighty-three.

The first I know of my own line
Was not in Dorset bred:
He, coming down from Closworth,
A Martinstown girl wed.

I don't know what his roots were:
In Somerset or here,
For Slades had been in Martinstown
A hundred years before.

The family was quite lowly,
In service or in toil
And never very holy:
In workhouse, but not gaol.

In eighteen seventy, one of us
Achieved some lasting fame
For when he took his wedding vows
Could sign and write his name!

From then on we could prosper
As well as scrimp and save
And Granddad had a proper
Stone to mark his grave!

My Father, at the village school,
When they were on parade,
With forty pupils it was full
And ten of them were Slade!

Father was at first a groom;
A gunner in the War,
Surviving many a blast and boom,
Field Regiment ninety-four.

He finished as a Sergeant
And then rejoined my Mam
And gardened for a local gent,
Then laboured on a farm.

His children: Brother, Sis and me
Are scattered far afield.
Brother's now in Yeovil; he's
Near Closworth: ain't that weird?

My Mother, in her nineties,
Was living in a home.
Each year upon her birthday
We'd all meet in Martinstown.

Father died some years ago
In nineteen ninety-four
Now it's time for Mum to go.
They'll meet at Heaven's door.

BRICK

I contemplate an ancient brick;
its face part hid by mossy beard.
A part is missing, crumbled, gone.
Was it once part of some great house
that was demolished long ago,
or just an easeance set outdoors?
It matters not whate'er it was
as, like its maker, long before,
it came at first from common clay
and that's how it will end some day.

GRIME'S GRAVES

Arrival and check-in at the desk-cum-shop.
The lady is friendly and helpful.
She offers me a sample of nettle wine:
must get the recipe!

To the pit on show:
Hard hats on and a slow descent
down steps to where, not long ago,
children played at hide and seek.

The linking tunnels now are barred
But one can see the bounty:
massive flints, two or three pecks,
unlike the fist-sized stones at home.

Aloft again, to wander on the plain;
pimpled and dimpled with pits and humps.
Cuckoos cry, the first I've heard this year.
More skylarks than ever I have seen at once
speak with each other and with me.

Apart from them, the silence is profound:
no engine-hum or man-made sound,
save for the tinnitus in my head.

I look around. The sheep-cropped turf
displays more tiny, grassland flowers
than I have seen since, when a child,
I played near the local chalk pit.

The wind is gentle,
the multitude of blobs of cloud
slow moving.

I find a pit, recline, and watch
the clouds drift by above.
Gradually the tinnitus fades
and so do I.

MARLENE SANDERSON

AFTER THE WAR

My house is built of rubble,
my rooms furnished with stones,
small pieces for chairs,
one large piece for my table.

My garden is planted with
willowherb, dandelion and privet.
My view is of the Lyons Corner House
damaged by bombs.

I am a builder.

THE EXCITEMENT OF IT ALL,

the City,

four-inch heels,

passion fruit,

married man.

LA RETRAITE DE
MONSIEUR RENARD, OR THE
RETIREMENT OF MR. FOX

Men say pride precedes a fall.
Now here's a tale to warn us all.

Monsieur Renard, Parisian Fox
Decides to step outside the box.

This city slicker – in his prime –
Relinquishes his life of crime.

He's tired of garlic-favoured dishes
From upturned bins in chic French cities.

Boards a ship in nearby Caen,
Sails to England, buys a farm.

His purchase is in Cattistock.
He settles down to count his flock.

While Renard wallows in this reverie,
Shepherd raises gun so cleverly,

Shoots old Foxy up the arse
And sends him flying through the grass.

Skin and hair from that old brush
Rain down upon each flowering bush

Where Renard now resides forever
Behind a hill of purple heather.

BLYTON

The child has measles.
The bedroom is sparse.
In the grate lumps of coal
burn for the invalid.

The child is bored.
She longs for the freedom
of the backyard.

She pulls the quilt over
her head, clicks on the torch
and takes herself to Faraway Tree,
Saucepan Man, Moonface,
Daffodil Biscuits, Popping Candy.

ELAINE BECKETT

AS WHISPERED TO A TENT

We are laying you out again
as flat as can be over new mown grass
on this blazing hot summer's day,
more beautiful than imagined
with the clock tower about to strike three
and the hazy threat of a downpour overhead,
whether or not there is anything left to say.

I hold your poles tight as he pegs you down,
wait for him to balance,
lean to stop you tipping into lettuces,

the willow tree grown thicker now,
enter your sweet-smelling dome
with its memories – so fresh
they turn me to love.

SITUATIONS LIKE THIS

There are reed beds, there are rafts made of reeds,
some can be waded through, others signify death,
you wouldn't risk floating them out on the water if it were dark.
It is memories that count in situations like this –
at the edge of the shore,
no-one about, light falling away,
shadows lengthening,

shadows lengthening,
no-one about, light falling away
at the edge of the shore.
It is memories that count in situations like this –
you wouldn't risk floating them out on the water if it were dark,
some can be waded through, others signify death.
There are reed beds, there are rafts made of reeds.

SOMETHING PINK

A flurry of sleet,
blowing in from God knows where –
or is it hail

spatters the cellophane
that holds my six bright tulips,
cheerful with possibilities.

Something pink
to put next to the absence
on the mantelpiece.

THE WOMAN WHO CRIES

(by Pablo Picasso)

It arrived in a clean white envelope
stamped Rotterdam,
as if he were trying to gain perspective.

I'd hoped for a neutral image –
a canal, a piece of Delft
but the message read:

don't be *La Femme Qui Pleure* –
and underneath, he'd underlined the title.

So I turned the card over and there she was:
fractured, pitiful, a red-and-blue lifeboat lodged
in her hair, driven mad by her own salt waters.

I kept her close to me for days,
until I began to feel grateful,

grateful for knowing such a man,
a man who could match me to a painting
that summarised the trouble we were in.

NIGHT NURSE
(for Geraldine)

Thinking of later
when a word like *orange*
can be taken to the limit,
she pours out his squash,

reminds him he'll be ninety-two
next week, tucks in his sheet,
revives the chrysanthemum
left by his son.

Bar emergencies,
with everyone asleep,
she will unfold the word,
enjoy its nuances, its relations,
its quirky connotations

and later still
she'll lay out the trays,
and notice how the colours
of marmalade differ.

LIZ FLIGHT

I KNOW I PROMISED NO ELEPHANT POEMS, BUT

do you remember those 3D pictures
so popular in the nineties?
You stared hard at them,
until your eyes watered and things went blurry,
you stared harder through your tears.
Then the object appeared.

This is what happens
when you spot elephants in the wild.
You stare at the place you know they should be -
the dried-up bed of the Ugab River –
you look hard, then harder, then
from nowhere, they appear.

THIS IS
MY SONG
ABOUT DRINK

He comes to avoid being alone.
She comes to be all on her own.
He comes on his own to meet someone.
She comes on the chance he'll be the one.

He comes to brag.
She comes to lie.
They come to sing.
Why does she cry?

They come to chat.
He comes to row.
She comes to sit in silence.

They come to put the world to rights.
He comes to fuel the family fight.
She comes to get away, to run.
Thirst is never why they come.

BAD NEWS IS BEST

Are you phoning about Claire? she said.
You must remember Claire from school.
She stabbed her baby to death last week,
then drank antifreeze, then slit her throat.
She was in your class, remember?
Oh yeah, she's dead, a good thing too.
So why did you call?

UNDER-ACTIVE GLANDS

An inhaler hangs around his neck,
a medal to earn him ultimate respect
and it swings to and fro as he waddles on through
breathlessly finding a table.

He can't move any further so I have to approach
him to establish what it is he wants for his lunch
and the beads of sweat and his beetroot head
almost distract me from what's being said.

No nuts, no wheat, no dairy, no meat –
shellfish unthinkable, fruit indigestible –
and if he's presented with a vegetable quiche
a coughing fit will never cease.

The lecture and lists go on and on
and the kitchen must pay close attention
because the only thing that won't cause him to choke
is deep-fried cod, chips, ketchup and coke.

SARAH BARR

AUTUMN IN VENICE

I don't remember anyone talking to us
apart from shopkeepers and waiters

the whole time we were there.
We hardly talked to each other

though there were things we could have said.
You bought me a glass-and-gold necklace.

Overnight water crept into the square;
Efforts to save this city ebb and flow.

The water, beautiful with reflections,
stinks in August though less so in November.

We trod up and down narrow streets
trying to reach our destination.

The alley-ways looked different
coming the other way.

We stumbled into an old ghetto.
We forgot why we'd come to Venice

or what we'd intended to do with our days
between houses like crumbling wedding-cakes,

shop windows crammed with masks
and stiff-limbed, velvet-dressed dolls.

SINGAPORE NIGHT ZOO

Black bushes, blacker grass,
a night without stars or moon,

the animals are silent,
still as illustrations

in a children's picture-book -
a mottled giraffe, leggy hyenas,

dusky lions, tiny mouse-deer
hidden by leaves,

a fishcat dipping its paw
into a pool,

a rhinoceros with tusks,
elephants too large for their page.

Don't photograph or feed them.
Talk only in whispers.

Like childhood fears,
these shadow-shapes loom,

separated from us by ditches
and flimsy fences.

TRYING TO STAY IN THE HERE AND NOW

Really tasting this coffee,
I see the embroidered lilac purse
dropped on the café floor
and hear the young woman say,
I'll hand it in at the counter.

Glossy fan-shaped leaves
of the plant by my table
remind me of a holiday
in the Indian Ocean.
I'm trying to stay in the here and now.

A man sitting nearby has one child
draped across his knee, the other grins
over a glass of hot chocolate,
her big teeth serrated and new.
She's wearing turquoise ear-muffs.

Lacquer-red lampshades
and door-frames look Chinese,
remind me of my mother's Mah Jong set,
also the Great Wall of China
that can be seen from Outer Space.

In the newspaper I've spread out on the table –
a photo. Now I'm thinking of flamingos,
hundreds of them flocking on a lake
when we cycled round the Camargue
and the wild white horses, galloping away.

MY MOTHER'S FRIENDS' DAUGHTERS

I did not look forward to
the arrival of these girls I didn't know
who were often bossy, spoilt, or very, very shy.
'Can't you just take them
away, to the garden, play.
Don't do anything silly.'

But I liked skinny Anna,
her straight unkempt hair, the way
she didn't care about her plain boy's clothes
and although polite how she seemed
casually indifferent
to the rules of my family life.

She arrived haphazardly
just once, one school holiday,
the daughter of poor Meryl
who worked as a live-in housekeeper
and was a single parent although
I never heard that said.

With Anna, I was allowed to
go to a screening of 'Old Yeller'.
Shocked by the story of a dog's death,
walking back in the dusk,
we were linked by sadness.
She was willing to fit in

with anything I wanted to do,
even making plaster models,
painting and varnishing
these lumpy creations in my bedroom,
secretly. And so, a few days later,
when she'd gone home

and the patch of varnish
I'd spilt on my blue plaid bedcover
was found to have hardened
it was easy, just for once, to escape blame
and whisper, 'I didn't want to say at the time
but that was done by Anna.'

ST. GREGORY'S

Silver-tipped bottles
glisten in their crates –
one third of a pint is a lot
if you hate milk.

Warming up, going off,
slurp it down, use a straw.
I try and get someone else
to drink mine.

The stink of milk
goes with damp wool.
pee, inky fingers, dust,
dead flowers and greasy hair.

I'm slow to fit in
at primary school,
glad when illness
exempts me

from this creamy poison
so I can have orange –
clear, sharp, sunny,
like being on holiday.

STEVE WAREHAM

A SONNET:
FOR A COUNTRY GENTLEMAN

Once a week I mowed his lawn,
the old man who lived down the lane,
a gentle man whose death we mourn,
cheered by the sun, cheered by rain.
His eye for detail was beyond measure;
a butterfly collection, lovingly framed,
fields he combed for schoolboy treasure,
sun or moon, wax and wane.
I loved to know him; our time was brief.
As we raise a loving cup of grief,
he's stalking deer, tickling trout
and with the beaters driving out,
and know that all these things must pass
like fallen leaves upon his grass.

HER GLORIOUS DAYS

I remember death's growing impatience
curling her lip in an impostor's smile,
and me, marooned on a plastic chair,
left to decipher movement,
muscle spasms, twitches of recognition.

Had the torrent of her glorious days
held her above the surface?
Is the surge sweeping her away
to shoot the narrow rapids
we fear to negotiate?

Her fight went all the way.
Why wouldn't she throw in the towel?
To keep dad a safe distance from the pub?
Because the bathroom would lose its shine?
There'd be no Christmas cards this year.

Now the world's outgrown her.
What did she know of cold callers, Al Qaeda,
chavs, morning-after pills, civil partnership,
the thumbscrews of modern life
(where terms and conditions apply)

and that her golden boy had fleeced her,
never coming up with the goods,
leaving her empty-handed,
short-changed by deaths and resurrections
she didn't live to see.

GENERATION GAME

I see her with a Mackeson's,
on her lap a plate of tripe,
watching Brucie on the box,
no surfaces to wipe.
Anthea gave us a twirl;
The old lady remembered a girl:
When I met your granddad I was that thin.
My hair was like silk, so was my skin.

She filled me with folklore, old superstition,
part common-sense, part intuition,
old wives' tales, sayings and fables,
broken mirrors, black cats, shoes on tables
and got to the bottom of what's in your heart,
told me a fool and his money soon part,
neither a borrower nor a lender be –
still ring out like alarm bells to me.

Her kindness still clings, close as a shroud.
I almost hear her talking out loud.
I can smell the nasturtiums,
loose tea with laughter,
where an hour's sleep before midnight's
worth more than two after.
Glued to the Generation Game,
babysitting her boy,
hostess trolley, fondue set, toaster, cuddly toy.

MANCUNIAN BALLS

It was seventy-nine back in my prime
I clapped eyes on John Cooper Clarke.

At the Victoria Hall he stood thin and tall
rhyming words like bird and turd.
I thought I can do this,
I can rhyme kiss with piss.
There's power in the spoken word.

He's got some bottle, mouth at full throttle,
a shock of electrified hair;
straight from the gob,
he force-fed the punk mob
with a pale Roy Orbison stare.

With Mancunian Balls
he milked the cat calls –
phlegm flew like moths in the spot.
A two-fingers style, a sarcastic smile,
and an exit with Right, that's yer lot!

Years down the line, penning this rhyme
I ask myself what made me start?
Was it obsessive, regressive,
or just plain excessive,
a download straight from the heart?

Is it now an affliction,
my twilight addiction,
a scab to bridge over the hole?
I don't know why I started to try
but I'll tell you what once left a mark:

It was seventy-nine back in my prime
I clapped eyes on John Cooper Clarke.

MY EYES ARE OPENED WIDE

When the wind is hunting trophies
on days not fit for dogs,
I see the savage breakers
exploding at The Cobb.

The dew clings ever longer,
the shadows grow and wilt,
and jewels bead the lavender
on threads of anchored silk.

The borders drain of colour,
the flocks desert the sky,
and swarms that scraped the barrel
have drunk the nectar dry,

and though I mark a change
with the absent dragonflies,
it's in the hour of darkness
my eyes are opened wide.

LISA STORM-OLSEN

MY CANALETTO

"Go fish" you cried,
as we snapped over
cards in a hasty pile.
The feverish wool
of our July blanket
laid us out like
lazy counters
on a chequer board
for larger beasts.

The divine hours
were elastic.
My pockets laden
with the currency of time.
Room to simmer water
for tea, read belly-down,
trim guy ropes and doze.

In the silence,
there was something loud;
My Canaletto –
peopled by nature,
its detail and colour
richly drawn.

AS EYE, AS TREE

after **Young Tree on Lewesdon Hill** *by Kit Glaisyer*

Moth-like,
        you are drawn
into this reservoir of light.

You're pouring into the canvas,
inhabiting this tree,
pressing your fingers against
the core, its Braille,
free from the desire for symmetry.

Only the freedom to feel
weather in all its textures,
cutting your pattern into the sky.

You reach
        the edges of the canvas,
but the lattice of branches
holds you in.

Light,
       haloing out,
diffuses into the paling particles,
brushed with silica, linseed oil,
turpentine
       and you're treacling
into the alchemy of it all, becoming
the molten body of colour.

You are totemic, solitary.

Listen —
       can you hear the sub-song
of an infant nightjar, or is that your own
heart beating?

The canvas
       has absorbed all sound —
it's your own music you hear
as the sun's eye in its gimbal
warms your rush of leaves.

You wait for the forest to still
that low frequency beat.

       You slip
out of the canvas and step
back into the room.

SUM

If he were to ask her to explain
what she'd done, the sum
of what she'd become,
could she trace every meander,
each brush with fresh shoot to yellow pass?
It would take a lifetime.
She doesn't have a lifetime.

She likes her minutes unmeasured.
And some things are lost in space,
and better that way, and others
are best seen through the telescope.

And while he is netting ideas,
making sharp manoeuvres
in a form of drive-by knowledge,
the rapids tunnelling him past the bank,
details blurred, she's punting
through the memories, upright as reeds,
feeling the division and shift of them –

the way one side is smooth,
the other jagged. All the time
watching the eddies and shinings
in the surface, and making a quill
from the feather of a swan's back.

And they're two amongst us.
Ranged like cabbages in allotments;
roundly squatting,
observed and tested,
waiting for the harvest.

CARRIE'S HOUSE

Carrie's house, yet to be condemned, teetered
on the cliff top. We played in the sun-room,
its windowsills littered with dead insects.
Our fathers, both absent, her with a new one,
me without. The memory of that

August – its layers of heat fusing
events with the burning sand.
A weaver fish delivered its brutal dart –
the pain like a needle as I made
the barefoot retreat on hot tarmac.

There were no tender daisies on the sea cliff.
No *love me, love me not.*
We grew inside a girdle of sea-holly, thrift
and wild evening primrose –
all leggy grace in its daytime composure,
only later at dusk its scent so heady.

ANNIE FREUD

BUJOLD

She marries him in a 'marriage blanc'
so that he can get a work permit.
He is an intellectual in disguise
and there is every kind of impediment:

the ambitious local cop in dark glasses
and leather jacket, determined to hound them,
her saucy younger sister, the absurd mother
giving a huge white wedding nobody wants.

At forty, she is ravishing in a haggard way;
and he looks seedy with his too-long hair;
there are some good jokes about lonely, frightened
people trapped in forced proximity:

'I know this place is a mess, but don't touch anything.
I know where everything is.' 'The cafetière is complicated.'
Love prevails in the end. We never see them
in bed and they only ever kiss at the wedding.

THE REMAINS

Tonight, my subject matter is the Fall of Rome
and I see a purple cloud in the empty street.

I was always of the slave mentality, but I talked
above my station.

I'm the peasant that killed the goose that laid
the golden eggs. The mermaid who sold her tail

for a pair of feet and ended up walking on knives.
The princess who chose the wrong casket.

You said you swore you'd never drive to a wedding
with your jacket on a hanger in the back

and now look at you. It's the same with me.
Every day I drink my coffee from this little cup

that I found in a job lot. Beauty, beauty, beauty,
I'd rather die than let go of her.

THE CATTISTOCK POETS

Nick Morris has lived in Dorset for most of his life. He's been an organist, piano teacher, copywriter and graphic designer, but has always written poetry and music in his spare time

Maya Pieris moved to Dorset with her family and food business in 2010. She has had a prose piece, and a photograph, included in Dorset Voices and has found contributing to this pamphlet an exciting experience.

Chris Slade, 'Dorset born, Dorset bred...' lives in Maiden Newton, a mere 23 minute walk from the Fox and Hounds. He wrote his first poem, a sonnet, at the turn of the Millennium. Most of his poems are linked with bee-keeping, his hobby/obsession, and he has a collection of them in preparation.

Marlene Sanderson was born in the Northwest of England and educated at Rochdale Convent Grammar School. She married in 1962 and had three daughters. She moved to Gloucestershire in the 1970s and to Wiltshire in 2007. She joined Annie Freud's poetry group in 2009.

Elaine Beckett has a background in music, film and architecture. Her poems have been shortlisted for the Bridport Prize in 2010 and 2011. Her poem 'For Roy' won the Bridport Prize's Dorset Award in 2012 and was published in the Bridport Prize Winners Anthology. A poem of hers will appear in *South Bank Poetry* Issue 17.

Elizabeth Flight studied for her BA in English Literature at Bangor University. She grew up in Manchester and can be described as a 'blunt, no nonsense Northener'. She loves travelling and has spent a lot of time in Canada, America and Africa. She is the landlady of the Fox and Hounds.

Sarah Barr writes about relationships, the natural world, loss and hope. She teaches creative writing in Dorset and for the Open University, gives readings and runs writing workshops. Her poetry and short fiction have been published in various magazines and anthologies. She was a Bridport Prize winner in 2010 and a South profiled poet in Issue 43.

Steve Wareham began writing in his late thirties. Now, at forty-eight, his range of influences is forever widening, from John Clare to John Cooper Clarke, Beowulf to Bob Dylan and beyond. He is a talented live performer of his work.

Lisa Storm-Olsen lives in Somerset with her son. One of her poems was shortlisted for the Bridport Prize in 2012 and she is currently studying for an MA in Creative Writing at Bath Spa University. She has had work published on the Bath Literature Festival website, has read poems on Bridport Radio, performs regularly at live events and was part of a Creative Works exhibition at the Museum of Bath at Work in 2013. She is working on her first collection of poems, Vermilion.

Annie Freud's first full collection, 'The Best Man that Ever Was' (Picador 2007) was awarded the Dimplex Prize for New Writing – Poetry in 2007. 'The Mirabelles' (Picador 2010), her second collection, was a Poetry Book Society Choice and was shortlisted for the TS Eliot Prize 2011. Her poems have been widely published in magazines and anthologies. She teaches poetry composition and is renowned for her live performances.